W9-DGI-573

THE

TEMPLE OF AMERICAN HISTORY

NATIONAL
ARCHIVES
BUILDING

BY
Patty Reinert Mason

FOREWORD BY
Adrienne Thomas
ACTING ARCHIVIST OF THE UNITED STATES

Thora Colot
Foundation for the National Archives, Washington, DC
EXECUTIVE DIRECTOR

Christina Gehring
Foundation for the National Archives, Washington, DC
PROJECT MANAGER

Maureen MacDonald
National Archives and Records Administration, Washington, DC
COPYEDITOR

Patty Reinert Mason
Foundation for the National Archives, Washington, DC
WRITER

Carol M. Highsmith & Colin Winterbottom
PHOTOGRAPHERS

Legendre + Rutter
DESIGNERS

Joanna & Declaration Script
TYPOGRAPHY
The font, Declaration Script, is based on the handwriting in the Declaration of Independence. The Joanna text font was designed by Eric Gill in 1930, the same year John Russell Pope was hired to design the National Archives Building.

2

Copyright © 2009 The Foundation for the National Archives, Washington, DC

ALL RIGHTS RESERVED
No part of the contents of this book may be reproduced, stored in a retrieval system, or transmitted in any form or by any means, without the written permission of the Foundation for the National Archives, Washington, DC.

Library of Congress Cataloging-in-Publication Data

Mason, Patty Reinert.
  The National Archives Building : temple of American history / by Patty Reinert Mason ; foreword by Adrienne Thomas.
    p. cm.
  ISBN 978-0-9758601-9-9
  1. National Archives Building (Washington, D.C.) 2. Washington (D.C.)--Buildings, structures, etc. 3. Pope, John Russell, 1874-1937. 4. Architects--United States--Biography. 5. Public buildings--Washington (D.C.)--Design and construction--History--20th century. I. Title.
  F204.N18M36 2009
  975.3--dc22
                                    2009034459

Manufactured in the United States of America
First Edition

FRONT COVER: **Embossing of the "Destiny" pediment, Pennsylvania Avenue, based on the photograph by Colin Winterbottom.**

CONTENTS

I	FOREWORD	5
II	INTRODUCTION	9
III	HISTORY	19
IV	THE ARCHITECT	27
V	THE PRESIDENT-ARCHIVIST	39
VI	LOCATION	49
VII	DESIGN AND CONSTRUCTION	59
VIII	SYMBOLISM	79
IX	SOMETHING'S MISSING	124
X	ACKNOWLEDGMENTS	126

Years before the first Archivist of the United States was appointed—indeed, before the National Archives and Records Administration even existed—architect John Russell Pope and his team were busy drawing up plans for the National Archives Building. Since its opening in 1935, this magnificent neoclassical revival building has drawn researchers and visitors from around the globe who have come to research their own family histories and to explore the important documents that helped build our nation.

Home to the original Charters of Freedom—the Declaration of Independence, the Constitution of the United States, and the Bill of Rights—the National Archives Building is where we safeguard our most valuable records and share them with each other, to learn from our history and to exercise our democratic duty to hold our Government accountable.

This book, produced by the National Archives' non-profit partner, the Foundation for the National Archives, is intended as a lay person's guide to the National Archives Building, explaining its history, its architectural features, and the symbolism of its many sculptures. It also explores the life and career of Pope, the role of President Franklin D. Roosevelt in the construction of the building and of the agency, and the contributions of the talented sculptors and stone carvers who not only gave this building its impressive decorations, but also conveyed its purpose and its significance.

During a major renovation from 2000 to 2005, Pope's historic building was updated and made more accessible to the public. Preservation work was completed on the Charters of Freedom, and Barry Faulkner's beautiful murals were painstakingly removed, restored, and reinstalled in the building's Rotunda.

The National Archives, working with the Foundation, also created the National Archives Experience with its award-winning Public Vaults, a permanent interactive educational exhibition that showcases many of the other treasures that can be found at the National Archives.

Today the building also houses the Lawrence F. O'Brien Gallery, displaying temporary and traveling exhibits highlighting the diversity of American records, and the 294-seat William G. McGowan Theater, which has become Washington's premier venue for documentary films, author lectures, and high-profile panel discussions.

In addition, the Boeing Learning Center, which opened in the building in 2007, is the flag-ship venue for National Archives education outreach, including interactive visitor programs, teacher training, student lab activities, distance learning, and Internet initiatives.

As the National Archives marks its 75th anniversary as a Federal agency, we celebrate our growth from this building, first occupied in 1935, to a nationwide network of facilities that today includes the National Archives at College Park, Presidential libraries and museums, regional archives, Federal records centers, and the *Federal Register*, as well as a presence in cyberspace.

We invite you to explore the place where it all began—John Russell Pope's masterwork: THE NATIONAL ARCHIVES BUILDING.

Adrienne Thomas

ACTING ARCHIVIST OF THE UNITED STATES

WEL
CO
ME
to
the
AR
CHI
VES

INTRODUCTION

President Hoover lays the cornerstone in 1933. Inside are a Bible, a U.S. flag, and copies of the Declaration of Independence and the Constitution.

"THIS TEMPLE OF OUR HISTORY
WILL APPROPRIATELY BE ONE OF
THE MOST BEAUTIFUL BUILDINGS
IN AMERICA, AN EXPRESSION OF
THE AMERICAN SOUL. IT WILL BE
ONE OF THE MOST DURABLE, AN
EXPRESSION OF THE AMERICAN
CHARACTER."

Herbert Hoover

PRESIDENT

Cornerstone Ceremony, February 20, 1933

11

The structure is massive—and grand. Viewed from the National Mall, it's clear this great vault, with its towering Corinthian columns, hand-carved pediments and allegoric sculptures, is so much more than a government office building or records warehouse.

To John Russell Pope, the architect who designed it, the National Archives Building was to be a temple to American history, a place where citizens would grasp the significance of and pay homage to democracy. Visitors were to ascend a colossal staircase to a columned portico, pass through the largest sliding bronze doors in the world, then through a set of spear-topped gates to enter a magnificent domed Rotunda soaring 75 feet. Once inside, they would gaze in awe upon the Charters of Freedom and other cherished documents enshrined in altar-like cases and flanked by huge murals depicting the Founding Fathers assembling a nation.

Designing the building in the early 1930s—years before the National Archives existed as an agency—Pope helped select the site, halfway between the White House and the U.S. Capitol, and insisted that only a monumental building in his beloved neoclassical style could appropriately showcase the most treasured documents of our democracy. He drew the building to be taller than its neighbors, surrounded it with a dry moat, and set it at an angle, all to impress upon passersby the importance of the building, not only to Washington's cityscape, but to the American people.

Many hailed Pope's masterwork as one of the most significant neoclassical revival buildings of the time. Yet some of the architect's modernist contemporaries and architectural critics openly attacked him, dismissing him as a "dinosaur" and ridiculing the ornate building as well as his plans for the nearby National Gallery of Art and the Jefferson Memorial. *Harper's Monthly* described Pope in 1934 as an architect who designed "equally brilliantly in all styles that are safely dead."

Regardless, the National Archives Building soon filled to the brim, and an interior courtyard Pope had designed for future expansion was almost immediately converted to stacks, doubling the building's storage space to nearly 800,000 cubic feet.

Besides the National Archives, which has occupied the building since 1935, the Office of Strategic Services, the nation's first central intelligence agency, also used some space in the building. Personnel from the Navy and the War Department worked in the building during World War II, making use of the National Archives' documents and maps as well as the building's enclosed courtyard—a "building within a building"—which was designated by the Government as a public bomb shelter and dubbed "Fort Archives" by the press. Hundreds of thousands of people visited the National Archives Building to see the Japanese and German surrender documents displayed in the Rotunda, just days after the fighting in each theater ended.

AT RIGHT: Seventy-two Corinthian columns surround the building. Each is 53 feet tall, 5 feet 8 inches in diameter, and weighs 95 tons.

Today, the National Archives holds for the American people billions of documents, photographs, maps, audio recordings and motion pictures. In addition to this building, "Archives II," the world's largest archival facility nestled into the woods of suburban Maryland, opened in 1994. The National Archives also encompasses dozens of regional archives, Federal records centers, and Presidential libraries. The nation's ever-growing collection of important records is secured around the country in a variety of buildings and even in rural caves. Increasingly, documents are being preserved digitally, and every year, more are made accessible via the Internet.

Still, 75 years after the National Archives was created, Pope's building in the heart of the nation's capital continues to draw more than a million visitors from around the globe each year. They come to research their family histories, to share our most precious national memories, and to examine the evidence of events we forget at our peril.

And as the home of the original Declaration of Independence, the Constitution of the United States, and the Bill of Rights, Pope's National Archives Building endures as he intended—as an inspiring shrine to American democracy. 🪶

War Department records stored in a White House garage before the National Archives was created.

IT IS WICKED THE WAY THESE FILES ARE STORED AND LEFT PELL MELL AT PRESENT.

Louis McHenry Howe

SECRETARY TO PRESIDENT FRANKLIN DELANO ROOSEVELT

letter to Interior Secretary Harold Ickes, May 18, 1934

Many Federal records were poorly stored until they reached the Archives.

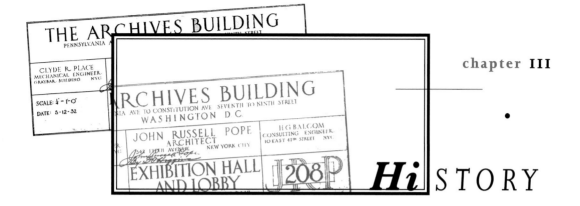

Long before the United States was a nation, record keepers understood the importance of documenting our history and safeguarding important papers. Detailed records were kept beginning with the first Continental Congress in Philadelphia in 1774, and during the American Revolution, as the Congress moved from city to city, official papers of the fledgling Government moved with it.

Later, records were sent to Washington where the permanent capital city had been established. During the War of 1812, as the British torched the White House and U.S. Capitol, officials

What
is past is
prologue

We the People

of the United States, in Order to form a more [perfect Union, establish Justice,] insure domestic Tranquility, provide for the common defence, promote the general Welfare, and secure the [Blessings of Liberty to ourselves] and our Posterity, do ordain and establish this Constitution for the United States of America.

Article. I.

Section. 1. All legislative Powers herein granted shall be vested in a Congress of the United States, which sha[ll consist of a Senate and House] of Representatives.

Section. 2. The House of Representatives shall be composed of Members chosen every second Year by the Peop[le] in each State shall have the Qualifications requisite for Electors of the most numerous Branch of the State Legislature.

No Person shall be a Representative who shall not have attained to the Age of twenty five Years, and been [a Citizen] and who shall not, when elected, be an Inhabitant of that State in which he shall be chosen.

Representatives and direct Taxes shall be apportioned among the several States which may be included within this [Union, according to their respective] Numbers, which shall be determined by adding to the whole Number of free Persons, including those bound to Service for a [Term of Years, and excluding Indians] not taxed, three fifths of all other Persons. The actual Enumeration shall be made within three Years after the first M[eeting of the Congress of the United States,] and within every subsequent Term of ten Years, in such Manner as they shall by Law direct. The Number of Represe[ntatives shall not exceed one for every] thirty Thousand, but each State shall have at Least one Representative; and until such enumeration shall be made, [the State of New Hampshire shall be] entitled to chuse three, Massachusetts eight, Rhode-Island and Providence Plantations one, Connecticut five, New Yo[rk six, New Jersey four, Pennsylvania] eight, Delaware one, Maryland six, Virginia ten, North Carolina five, South Carolina five, and Georgia three.

When vacancies happen in the Representation from any State, the Executive Authority thereof shall issue Writs [of Election to fill such Vacancies.]

The House of Representatives shall chuse their Speaker and other Officers; and shall have the sole Power of Imp[eachment.]

Section. 3. The Senate of the United States shall be composed of two Senators from each State, chosen by the Legisla[ture thereof, for six Years; and each] Senator shall have one Vote.

scrambled to salvage what they could, carting important records to the Potomac River and hauling them away on barges to safe houses.

As the national bureaucracy grew, its records eventually began piling up all over Washington. Some Federal agencies did a decent job of organizing and safeguarding documents; others did a terrible job, storing records in damp garages and basements, exposing them to humidity and bugs, or displaying them in public buildings where they were damaged by too much sunlight.

The Declaration of Independence was displayed opposite a window in the Patent Office for more than three decades before it was rescued and preserved. When historian J. Franklin Jameson, a founder and president of the American Historical Association, sought to examine the Constitution in 1883, he found it folded and stored in a small tin box in a closet at the State, War, and Navy Building.

Many other records were lost or stolen; some were sold as scrap paper or simply trashed. Fires were a constant threat in the 1800s and early 1900s. The 1890 Census was virtually destroyed, and other valuable records were damaged when fires broke out at the War Office, Treasury Department, Patent Office, and Commerce Department.

Veterans groups, historians, and architects hoping to remedy the problem proposed building a fireproof "Hall of Records," submitting their plans to everyone from the President on down. Congress studied the issue for decades, but did not approve funds for a National Archives Building until 1926.

AT RIGHT: Pope's other works in Washington include the Jefferson Memorial, the National Gallery of Art (West Building) and the Temple of the Scottish Rite (right).

The building was to be part of a new Federal Triangle development, which would provide office space for the expanding Federal Government while beautifying downtown Washington. In keeping with Pierre L'Enfant's original plan for the city as well as the 1901 McMillan Commission plan, the Government intended to clear the area north of the Mall, between Constitution and Pennsylvania Avenues, from 6th to 15th Streets, NW, which by the early 20th century was packed with factories, stores, hotels, and row houses.

Louis A. Simon, the supervisory architect of the Treasury Department, drafted a preliminary design for an archives building in the late 1920s, to be constructed on Pennsylvania Avenue between 9th and 10th Streets, NW. The Commission of Fine Arts panned it. They suggested that John Russell Pope, one of America's most prominent classical architects, be put in charge of the Archives Building.

Pope, who already had designed several residences and monumental buildings in Washington, including the award-winning Temple of the Scottish Rite and the Daughters of the American Revolution's Constitution Hall, was officially hired in 1930. It would be four more years before the National Archives itself was created by Congress and the first Archivist appointed, so Pope's vision for the building helped form the Government's vision for the National Archives. ⚜

Most of Pope's designs were drawn
by his partner Otto Eggers.

BUILDING FOR THE NATIONAL ARCHIVES

WASHINGTON D.C.

JOHN RUSSELL POPE ARCHITECT

"NEVER HAS THERE BEEN
ANYTHING SO ATTRACTIVE
PRESENTED TO ME BEFORE AND
NEVER HAS THE OFFICE BEEN

| S | O | | W | E | L | L |

| O | R | G | A | N | I | Z | E | D |

OR ABLE TO HANDLE IT."

John Russell Pope

Letter to Commission of Fine Arts, Chairman Charles Moore, July 11, 1928

26

chapter IV

*The Arc*HITECT

||||||||||||||||||||||||||||||||||||||||||||||||||||||||||||||||||||||||||||||||||||||||||||||||||||||

John Russell Pope was supposed to be a doctor, not an architect.

Born in New York in 1874, he was the son of John Pope, a respected portrait painter, and Mary Avery Loomis Pope, a piano teacher and landscape painter. When the elder John Pope died, "Jack" Pope was only 6 years old. He and his brother grew up with their mother and were heavily influenced by an uncle, a successful physician named Alfred Loomis.

A lasting imprint on the *nation's* capital

Pope enrolled at City College of New York as a teenager, and planned to transfer to medical school at The Johns Hopkins University in Baltimore after his sophomore year. Instead, he went to Columbia College (now Columbia University) to study architecture. Some said he changed his mind about following his uncle's career path after observing his first surgery; others noted that architecture was Pope's true calling because his best grades had always been in drawing, a skill that, in the era before widespread use of the camera, was considered critical for well-educated people in many professions.

After earning his Bachelor of Philosophy degree in architecture in 1894, Pope won two prestigious fellowships to study abroad and spent six years drawing the great buildings of Italy and Greece and studying at Paris' famed École des Beaux-Arts before returning home to New York. He was one of the first American architectural students to master the use of the large-format camera with glass negatives, and some of his building sketches from Europe include the notation "see photograph."

He returned to New York in 1900 with a portfolio of sketches, photographs, and watercolor paintings he used as inspiration and in discussions with clients and colleagues throughout his career. Pope eventually opened his own studio in New York and went to work designing homes for the wealthy, as well as grand buildings and monuments. Like many architects of his time, he supplemented his income in the early years by teaching.

At age 38, he married Sadie Jones, the 18-year-old daughter of wealthy socialites Pembroke and Sarah Jones and later, the stepdaughter of Henry Walters, a Baltimore railroad magnate and art collector. Though Pope's career was going well before he married, his wife's family connections brought his firm more work, mostly designing private residences. The couple had three daughters—Sarah, Mary, and Jane. Sarah died of meningitis at age 7, and Mary died in a car accident when she was a teenager.

A master of classical architecture and a leading proponent of the neoclassical style, Pope frequently used Roman design elements and symbols in his buildings, and was convinced that neoclassical architecture was the most appropriate style for public buildings in a democracy.

To his colleagues, Pope was a great collaborator with a well-ordered mind and a talent for seeing a huge, monumental building as a whole while also paying close attention to relatively minor design elements, insisting on detailed renderings of windows, light fixtures, and grates covering vents. He was a gifted draftsman, but often provided only the initial sketches, relying heavily on longtime partner Otto R. Eggers to produce the final drawings. Eggers, an excellent draftsman and well-respected architect in his own right, ran the New York office along with Pope's other longtime partner, Daniel Paul Higgins, whenever Pope was away—which was often.

To outsiders, Pope seemed aloof and reclusive, appearing to lose interest in many of his clients shortly after securing their contracts. He often

PAGES 31–34: **Floor plans for the Archives Building.**

declined to meet with those he disliked or didn't think worthy of his attention. He summered with his wife and family at their Newport, Rhode Island, home and studio, "The Waves," keeping in touch with his office but leaving most client relations to Eggers and Higgins. (Eggers struggled with a significant stammer, so he often drafted a junior designer to speak for him at such meetings.)

Pope snubbed even John D. Rockefeller, Jr., refusing to return to New York to present his drawings for The Cloisters. Rockefeller was furious and had the last word, awarding the contract to someone else.

Depressed over his daughter Mary's death and suffering from his own illnesses, Pope withdrew further in the 1930s, even as he produced designs for the high-profile National Archives Building and later, the National Gallery of Art (West Building) and the Jefferson Memorial.

Clinging to Neoclassicism at a time when other American architects were embracing Modernism and its mantra of "form follows function," Pope was increasingly criticized and isolated by his peers. His design for the art gallery, which Higgins and Eggers finished after Pope's death in 1937, was derided by one critic as "a Mausoleum for dead masters" and by another as "The Last of the Romans." Even after his death, Pope himself also was mocked with the nickname "Last of the Romans" and his reputation as a great architect crumbled.

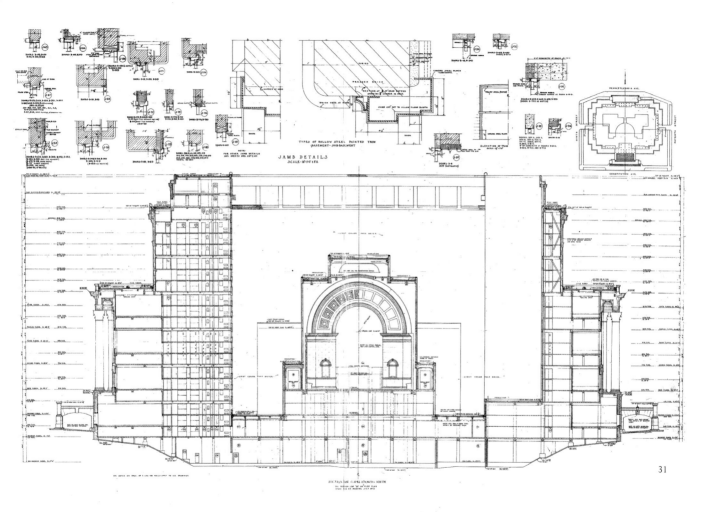

JAMB DETAILS
SCALE

31

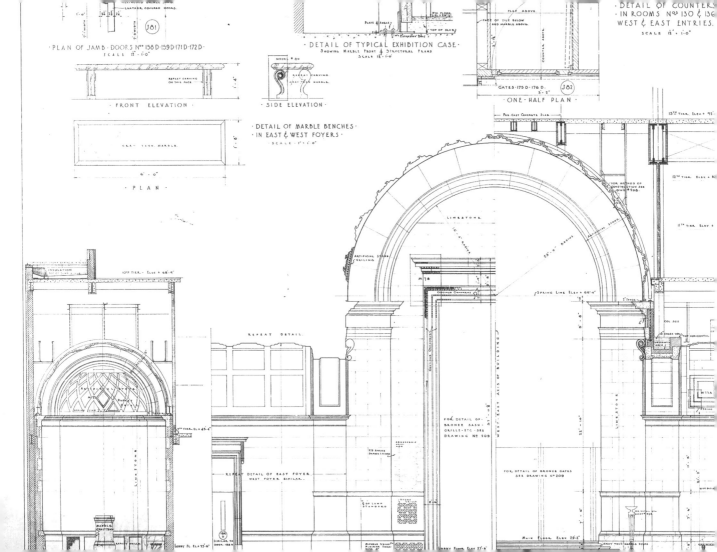

·PLAN OF JAMB · DOORS N°S 158 D·159 D·171 D·172 D·
SCALE 1½"= 1'-0"

· FRONT ELEVATION ·

GRAY TENN. MARBLE.

· PLAN ·

6'-0"

MODEL #80

SIDE ELEVATION ·

·DETAIL OF MARBLE BENCHES·
·IN EAST & WEST FOYERS·
· SCALE · 1"= 1'-0" ·

·DETAIL OF TYPICAL EXHIBITION CASE·
SHOWING MARBLE FRONT & STRUCTURAL FRAME
SCALE 1½"= 1'-0"

·DETAIL OF COUNTERS·
·IN ROOMS N°S 130 & 136·
WEST & EAST ENTRIES·
SCALE 1½"= 1'-0"

· ONE · HALF · PLAN ·
GATES· 175 D· 176 D·
3'-2"

LIMESTONE

SPRING LINE ELEV + 66'-0"

FOR DETAIL OF
BRONZE SASH
GRILLE ETC SEE
DRAWING N° 208

REPEAT DETAIL OF EAST FOYER·
WEST FOYER SIMILAR·

FOR DETAIL OF BRONZE GATES
SEE DRAWING N° 208

MAIN FLOOR ELEV 29'-2"

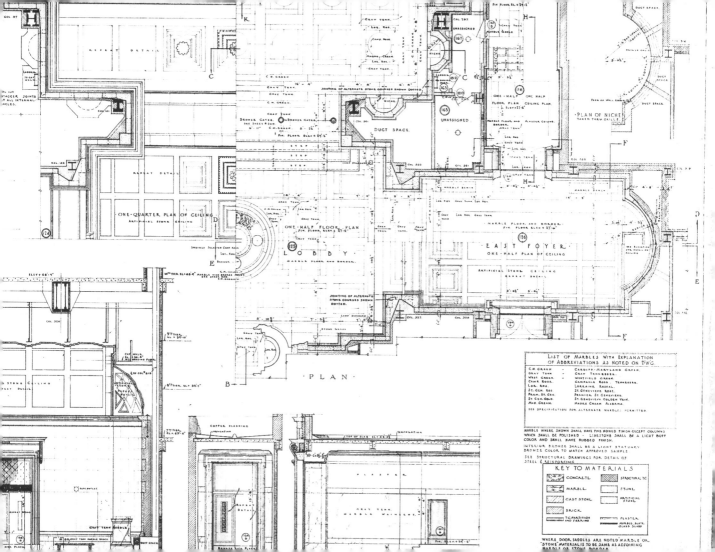

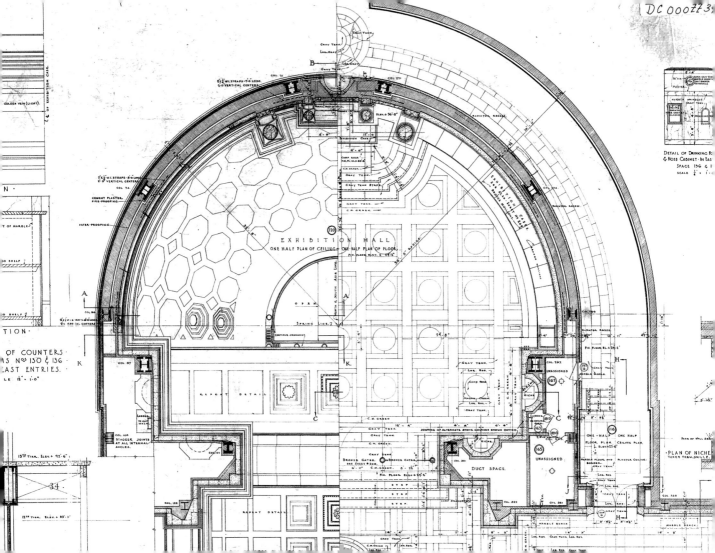

DC 000773

FOLLOWING PAGE: In James Earl Fraser's "Guardianship" statue on Constitution Avenue, a soldier with a plumed helmet, shield, and sword symbolizes protection. The quote beneath the sculpture reads: "Eternal vigilance is the price of liberty."

In a letter to President Franklin Delano Roosevelt in 1937, famed architect Frank Lloyd Wright complained that Pope's design for the Jefferson Memorial was an "arrogant insult to the memory of Thomas Jefferson." Architect William Lescaze called the memorial, which Pope had modeled on the Pantheon in Rome—one of architect Jefferson's favorite structures—"a flatulent adaptation of a second-rate Imperial Roman building." Even the faculty of the school of architecture at Columbia University, Pope's alma mater, critiqued the memorial as a "lamentable misfit in time and place."

The criticism of his work stung, yet Pope was proud of his monuments and monumental buildings, as well as his service to the nation as a member of the Board of Architectural Consultants on the Federal Triangle project and as a member of the Commission of Fine Arts. Though he won many architectural awards as a student and as a professional, Pope's studio waiting room in New York was adorned with two cherished documents: framed letters from Presidents Woodrow Wilson and Warren Harding, commending his public service and his work in Washington.

Pope died in 1937 of abdominal cancer. Today, he is considered one of America's best and most important classical architects. He designed more monumental buildings than anyone of his generation and left a lasting imprint on the nation's capital. ❧

To bring together the records of the past and to house them in buildings where they will be preserved for the use of men and women in the future, a nation must believe in three things. It must believe in the past. It must believe in the future. It must, above all, believe in the capacity of its own people so to learn from the past that they can gain in judgment in creating their own future.

Franklin Delano Roosevelt

PRESIDENT

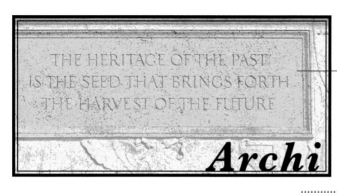

THE HERITAGE OF THE PAST
IS THE SEED THAT BRINGS FORTH
THE HARVEST OF THE FUTURE

Archi

chapter V

THE PRESIDENT-VIST .

To

learn

from

the

past

President Franklin Delano Roosevelt was a life-long collector of stamps, historic manuscripts, ship models, and books. He was a genealogist and historian and also fancied himself an archivist and an architect.

Taking office in March 1933, just two weeks after President Herbert Hoover laid the cornerstone to the National Archives Building, FDR inherited responsibility for a structure under construction and an agency yet to be created. During his early years in the White House, as he struggled to lead the nation through the Great

PREVIOUS SPREAD: **In James Earl Fraser's "Heritage" statue on Constitution Avenue, a woman holds a child and a sheaf of wheat symbolizing growth and hopefulness. In her left hand is an urn, symbolizing the ashes of past generations.**

Depression, the President directly oversaw the Archives building's construction, signed the bill creating the National Archives agency, and appointed the first Archivist of the United States.

He put his most trusted secretary and political confidant, Louis McHenry Howe, in charge of the project, and expressed his opinions on everything from the building's design to what types of records should be included in the National Archives and who should be hired to work there.

When it became clear the hulking building would not be big enough to house existing Federal Government records, FDR sent memos approving a plan to fill its courtyard with additional stacks sooner than had been anticipated.

John Russell Pope wrote to him—directly and through the President's cousin, Laura Delano, complaining that he was shut out of the courtyard in fill project. Delano forwarded Pope's concerns to the President, sending him a handwritten note. "Dear Franklin," she wrote, "Jack Pope loves this building as nothing he has ever created and does so want to finish it." Unmoved, FDR instructed a White House staffer to send Pope a rather dismissive reply, informing him that no further architectural services would be required.

A few months later, however, FDR personally intervened to protect Pope's overall design by barring the construction of a new sloping roof that was intended to provide even more stack space. In a memo to the Treasury secretary on March 6,

FOLLOWING SPREAD: The "Past" (left) and "Future" (right) statues on the Pennsylvania Avenue side of the building were designed by Robert I. Aitken, who also designed the pediment above the front entrance to the U.S. Supreme Court.

1935, the President wrote: "I wholly agree… that no new or higher roof should be placed on the Archives Building. Please keep the design of the outside as originally made by the architect."

FDR often consulted with Archivist R.D.W. Connor, offering advice on records storage methods and fireproofing as well as on the administration of the National Archives. "I hope you will consider the possibility of appointing a Negro to work on such archives as relate to the Negro race in the United States," he wrote to Connor in the mid-1930s. "I think it would be a valuable gesture if it is warranted by the need." Connor agreed.

The President, an incurable collector since childhood, favored erring on the side of saving virtually everything, saying he distrusted man's ability to foresee the value of any document to future generations. So committed was he to preserving the historical record, that he also protected enemy archives confiscated during World War II, dispatching archives advisors overseas to help with the effort. And, in the years before the atomic bomb, he issued warnings about the vulnerability of housing all of the National Archives' treasures in downtown Washington, saying the most important documents should be duplicated on microfilm and distributed around the country.

After listening to recordings of one of his fireside chats and an address before Congress, he urged Connor to archive audio records. He also pushed for the preservation of motion picture

41

films and fretted over their storage for fear that housing flammable film in the same building as so much paper posed too much risk. Connor agreed that film should be preserved, and today, the National Archives holds hundreds of thousands of motion picture film reels, video, and audio recordings.

FDR's insistence on archiving motion picture reels left a lasting mark on the Archives. The original building included a theater and today's state-of-the-art movie theater is home to the Charles Guggenheim Center for the Documentary Film.

FDR also fired off memos to his Cabinet whenever he felt they weren't taking the National Archives project seriously. On June 17, 1937,

he wrote to the secretary of war: "I am told that the Confederate records are stored in a garage on Virginia Avenue. Don't you think it would be a good idea to turn them over to the Archivist, Dr. Connor? He has room for them and it would take the cost of space and maintenance off the War Department."

Perhaps the President's most important contribution to the National Archives came in 1938 when Roosevelt announced he would build his own fireproof archive at his home in Hyde Park, New York, to store his Presidential and personal papers, which would be shared with the American people. By his death in 1945, the President's collections also included some 22,000 books, 1,200 naval prints and paintings, more than 200 ship models, and hundreds of historical manuscripts and ship logs. This gift to the nation set the precedent for the creation of Presidential libraries and museums.

Long before the FDR Memorial along Washington's Tidal Basin was dedicated in 1997, the President was honored as he hoped he would be—on the grounds of the National Archives Building. A plain marble monument the size of his White House desk is planted at the corner of 9th Street and Pennsylvania Avenue, NW. Per the President's wishes, it bears only a simple inscription: "In memory of Franklin Delano Roosevelt."

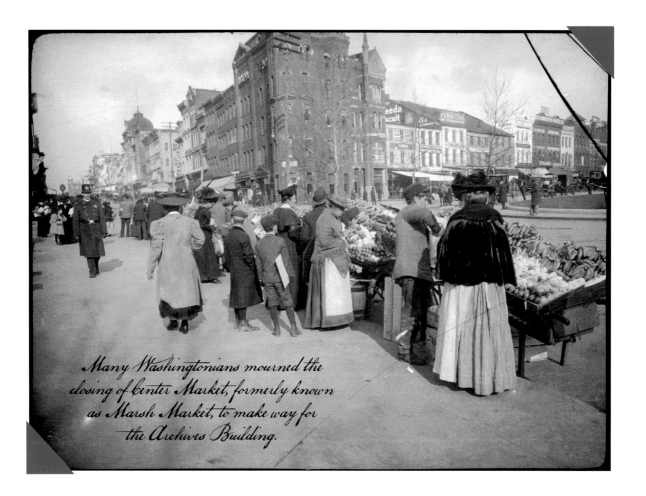

Many Washingtonians mourned the closing of Center Market, formerly known as Marsh Market, to make way for the Archives Building.

Indeed it is doubtful whether from the point of view of air, light, and safety from flood, there could be found a much worse site in the District of Columbia than the one on which it is now proposed to construct the Archives Building in the near future.

Samuel Flagg Bemis
HISTORY PROFESSOR AND ARCHIVES EXPERT
AT THE GEORGE WASHINGTON UNIVERSITY

letter to President Herbert Hoover, November 19, 1929

Pope insisted the Archives be located between 7th and 9th Streets, NW.

chapter VI

Center Market in 1928

•

*Loca*TION

|||||||||||||||||||||||||||||||||||||||||||||||||||||||||||||||||||||||||||||||||||||||||||||||||||||||||||||||||||||||||

Present-day Constitution Avenue runs along the National Mall side of the National Archives Building about where Tiber Creek used to flow. Early Washingtonians hunted birds along its banks, and in the 19th century, the creek was part of a canal system connecting the Anacostia and Potomac Rivers. Long after the marshy area was filled in and covered over, the eastern part of the National Mall was a rather soggy place to walk, let alone build.

In the early 1800s, a collection of stalls had nevertheless sprung up in the area and peddlers had

From
marsh
to market
to Archives

49

begun selling their wares and produce. "Marsh Market"—later Center Market—also served as a makeshift slave market before the trade was moved to nearby hotels.

By the early 1920s, Center Market had become the largest retail market in the District of Columbia for meat, fruit, and vegetables, and also housed a cold storage plant, a power plant, restaurant, auditorium, and offices. Hundreds of vendors operated inside the busy market, while local farmers sold their produce from trucks parked outside. Press accounts described the landmark as a place where Presidents' wives rubbed shoulders with "humbler shoppers," and where "congressmen have spent many a Saturday morning discussing the beef situation with its butchers." First Lady Julia Grant had done her own shopping at the market for parties at the White House. According to Jacob West, a long-time butcher at the market, "She was a nice lady, always pleasant, and she knew her business about buying meat." Presidents Garfield and Cleveland also frequented the market, as did President Theodore Roosevelt, accompanying his wife on weekly shopping trips and, according to C.H. Walleigh, superintendent of the market, "making sly remarks about her buying ability."

The Federal Department of Agriculture took over the market's operation in 1923, but by May 1928, the Government announced it would tear it down to make way for the Federal Triangle project, a development of Government office buildings from 6th to 15th Streets, NW, between Pennsylvania and Constitution Avenues, that was to include the National Archives Building.

Center Market was the most popular market in Washington. Its shoppers included Presidents and lawmakers.

Also pushed out of the way was Washington's original Chinatown, which used to hug Pennsylvania Avenue. After being displaced by the Federal Triangle project, Chinese immigrants moved their homes and businesses a few blocks north.

Early proposals for Federal Triangle placed the National Archives down the street, between 12th and 13th Streets, NW, between 9th and 10th Streets, NW, or between 10th and 11th Streets, NW. When Pope came aboard, he insisted the building's proper location was between 7th and 9th Streets, NW—the cross-axis of the city's monumental core as originally conceived by Pierre L'Enfant, the French-born American architect and civil engineer who designed the capital city.

Government planners had researched and visited archives around the world in hopes of learning from the successes and failures of others. But because many European archives were housed in ancient castles and government buildings originally constructed for other purposes, they found little help. As they were designing the world's first archives that would be built from scratch specifically to house and maintain mostly paper documents, Pope and his colleagues would have to go it alone.

Which is not to say that plenty of people didn't offer advice. For starters, many objected to Pope's proposed location for the building, warning that the low-lying area of the National Mall was prone to flooding and that humidity and insects would threaten the integrity of the valuable records. Amateur archivists and historians

PAGE 56: Detail of the pediment on the building's Pennsylvania Avenue side.

disagreed over whether precious documents should be exposed to fresh air and sunlight to prevent mold and mildew, or housed in a cool, dark space to keep the records from drying out and turning to dust.

Others argued that locating the building so near the White House and Capitol would make the National Archives Building a prime target for bombing in wartime. Many preferred locating the building high on a hill on the city's outskirts, or dividing the records and shipping them to various secret locations in the nation's interior.

"I believe the site tentatively selected would be a serious blunder, which would be lastingly regretted," Librarian of Congress Herbert Putnam warned in a letter to the Public Buildings Commission in January 1928.

In the end, Pope and his supporters had their way, moving the proposed Justice Department building out of the way and placing the Archives on two full blocks downtown, between 7th and 9th Streets, NW. Pope set the building back from Pennsylvania Avenue to draw attention to it and gave its occupants a perfect view across the avenue to the Greek revival U.S. Patent Office, which is now home to the Smithsonian National Portrait Gallery and American Art Museum.

Don't be fooled by the National Archives' address of 700 Pennsylvania Avenue. The building is exactly halfway between the U.S. Capitol and the White House at 1600 Pennsylvania Avenue. ❧

Construction site for Archives Building.

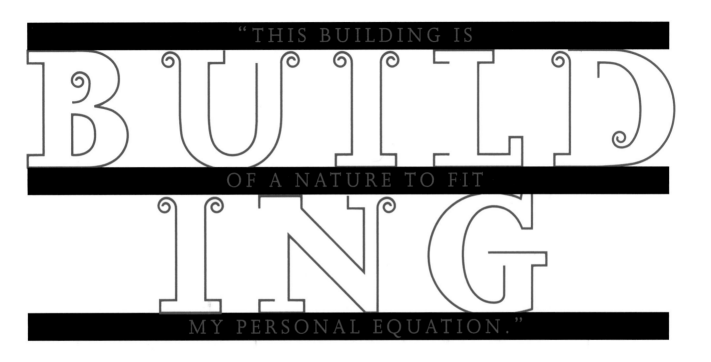

"THIS BUILDING IS
BUILD
OF A NATURE TO FIT
ING
MY PERSONAL EQUATION."

John Russell Pope

Letter to Commission of Fine Arts Chairman Charles Moore, July 11, 1928

NOV 2 1933

The National Archives Building measures 330' x 213' x 168' or 70,290 square feet. That's roughly equal to 32 homes of 2,200 square feet each.

No. 47 — Taken Nov. 2 1933
The Archives Building
Washington, D. C.
John Russell Pope, Architect
George A. Fuller Co., Builders

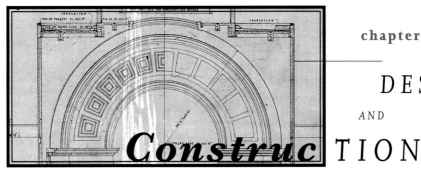

chapter VII

DESIGN

AND

TION
•

||||||||||||||||||||||||||||||||||||||||||||||||||||||||||||||||||||||||||||||||||

Pope's vision for the National Archives Building was to create not only a secure documents vault to house the nation's most valuable records, but also a national shrine to democracy itself.

As a neoclassical architect, he believed certain forms from ancient Greek and Roman architecture were inherently beautiful. Towering columns, carved pediments, and the all-important Rotunda were elements any neoclassical building would appear naked without. By relying on the neoclassical style, Pope said the building would "harmonize with the Capitol, White

What
makes
a building
neoclassical
?

59

House, Treasury Building, and the Lincoln Memorial," yet it would be by far the most ornate building in Federal Triangle. This was fitting, Pope said, because it would signal the unique and important role he believed the National Archives would play in American life.

His firm submitted its first design for the building in 1931. It was actually drawn by one of Pope's partners, Otto Eggers.

The building's granite exterior, surrounded by a dry moat and topped with six dozen Corinthian columns, was to resemble an enormous vault. The moat's walls would hide ground-floor office windows, adding to the building's secure appearance.

The Constitution Avenue entrance, through which most visitors would enter the building after climbing the grand staircase, would be shielded by the largest sliding bronze doors in the world. Carvings flanking the Pennsylvania Avenue entrance, where staff and researchers would enter the building, would depict armed "Guardians of the Portal," protecting the treasures inside.

The north and south sides of the building were to be topped by allegorical pediments that would be among the largest in the United States, each measuring 118 feet wide and 18 feet high at the peak. Four limestone statues atop granite pedestals, each measuring 13 feet by 8 feet by 10 feet and designed by some of the best sculptors of the time, would anchor the building.

Sculptors and carvers of the George Donnelly Company on the steps of the Archives in August 1934.

Sculptors & Carvers
Archives Building
Washington D.C.
August 1934

SEP 5 193

No. 40   Taken Sept. 5-1933
The Archives Building
Washington, D. C.
John Russell Pope, Architect
George A. Fuller Co., Builders

Construction in progress.

MAY 1 1934

GEORGE FULLER
COMPANY
BUILDING CONTRACTORS

No. 69   Taken May 1 1934
The Archives Building
Washington, D. C.
John Russell Pope, Architect
George A. Fuller Co., Builders

Buildings in the neoclassical style are monumental and grand. They include Greek or Roman detailing, dramatic columns, large porticoes, and allegoric pediments.

No. 88   Taken Sept. 4-1934
The Archives Building
Washington, D. C.
John Russell Pope, Architect
George A. Fuller Co., Builders

Pope also incorporated numerous carvings inspired by the ancient Greeks and Romans— goddesses of protection, lamps of knowledge, shields and swords of war, owls of wisdom, and eagles to represent valor and, of course, American strength.

Inside, the Rotunda's dome would hover 75 feet above the marble floor. Pope hoped visitors to the space would be awestruck, gaining "a proper realization of the significance and importance of the building itself as a complete record of the history of the National government." The National Archives' most treasured documents —including the Charters of Freedom—were to be displayed in the Rotunda beneath enormous murals depicting the founding of the nation.

There were also practical concerns. The building would require flooring reinforced in concrete and steel to support miles of shelving in the stacks and to bear the weight of billions of documents. The original building would have five 20-foot-high floors. (The interior courtyard, which was filled in with stacks shortly after the building opened, contains 21 7-foot-high floors.)

A fire suppression system was an absolute necessity in a building filled with paper, and the building's temperature and humidity would need to be controlled to protect documents from mold, mildew, and bugs. The National Archives would be among the first buildings in Washington with central air conditioning.

Pneumatic tubes would carry requests from a Central Research Room to archivists, who would retrieve and deliver the documents to waiting researchers.

Ground was broken on September 9, 1931, but construction, carried out by the main contractor, George A. Fuller Company of Washington, was far from easy. To support the weight of the massive building and its intended contents, workers from Frederick L. Crawford, Inc., a Brooklyn, New York-based construction company, drove 8,575 piles into the unstable marsh, then poured a concrete bowl 21 feet deep for the foundation.

Though Pope had specified that the building be constructed of granite, the country was in the midst of the Great Depression, and many lobbied to use less-expensive limestone. Pope, who considered limestone inferior, appealed to his Government clients for help. "This Archives will be for many reasons one of the most interesting and most important monuments in our great Washington plan," he wrote in 1933. "I naturally feel deeply my responsibilities in connection with it and the necessity of its having merit to the fullest and enduring quality as well." A compromise was struck: The base of the building would be made of granite; the rest of Indiana limestone.

The *Washington Evening Star* described Pope's building as an "impressive temple, honoring Clio," the muse from Greek mythology who presided over history. ✦

*The Archives Rotunda,
under construction*

No. 95 Taken Nov-2-193⁻
The Archives Building
Washington, D.C.
John Russell Pope, Architect
George A. Fuller Co., Builders

COST

In 1926, Congress appropriated
$6.9 million for the building.
The amount was later increased
to more than $8.5 million.

CONSTRUCTION
DATES

Ground was broken in 1931.
Parts of the building were
occupied by the fall of 1935,
but construction of the stacks
in the inner courtyard
continued through June 1937.

CORNERSTONE
CEREMONY

President Herbert Hoover lays the
building's cornerstone in 1933,
calling the building "an expression of the American soul."

COLUMNS

‖‖‖

The columns were completed in
sections and hoisted on top of
earlier sections. The capitals on
top were carved in place.

‖‖‖

DOORS

||||||||||||||||||||||||||||||||||||||||||||||||||||||||||||||||||||||||||||||

Visitors to the building originally climbed the grand staircase on Constitution Avenue
and walked through what were,
at the time, the largest bronze
doors in the world. Each door
weighs 6.5 tons and is 38 feet
7 inches high, nearly 10 feet
wide and 11 inches thick.
The doors slide to open and
therefore, can be seen only
when closed.

||||||||||||||||||||||||||||||||||||||||||||||||||||||||||||||||||||||||||||||

GUARDIANS OF THE PORTAL

Sculptor Robert I. Aitken's granite relief flanks the doors of the Pennsylvania Avenue entrance. Two Roman soldiers, one wearing a helmet, one wearing an animal skin, hold swords and shields and guard the doors leading to the nation's most important records. The burning flame behind each symbolizes "the heritage of the nation." The scroll in one soldier's hand may be the Declaration of Independence. Roman numerals carved behind each soldier are significant: MDCCLXXVI is 1776, the year the Declaration was signed; MCMXXXV is 1935, the year the Archives Building opened.

TEMPERATURE, HUMIDITY, LIGHT

Many visitors to the National Archives notice that the building is a bit chilly and the Rotunda a bit dim. The building's temperature, humidity, and light are controlled to help protect aging documents. In the stacks, the temperature is kept at a constant 68 degrees Fahrenheit and relative humidity is 45 percent. Lighting in the Rotunda is set at 2 foot candles—the light intensity of two candles placed one foot away. By comparison, natural light outdoors on a sunny day is about 12,000 foot candles.

FOLLOWING PAGE: **Detail from the flag pole.**

EMPTY NICHES

Four statuary alcoves in the Rotunda have been vacant since the building opened. It's unclear what statues Pope intended to place here.

sYMB**O**LISM

"IN VIEW
OF THE CLASSICAL SPIRIT
IN WHICH THE DESIGN OF
THE BUILDING WAS CONCEIVED,
IT WAS CONSIDERED ESSENTIAL BY THE
ARCHITECT AND THE SCULPTORS THAT
ALLEGORY RATHER THAN REALISM BE
THE MEANS OF CONVEYING THE
SIGNIFICANCE OF THE SCULPTURAL
DECORATION."

John Russell Pope,
1934

chapter VIII

Symbo LISM

Symbols are as important *as function*

As a neoclassical architect, Pope considered a building's appearance and symbolism to be as important as its function. He used symbols from Greek and Roman mythology inside and outside of the National Archives Building and spent more than $360,000 on the sculptural decorations—more than was spent on any other building in Federal Triangle. Washington's Federal Triangle alone contains more architectural sculpture than can be found in entire cities in the United States. Pope also took great care in selecting the building's artists and sculptors. His original sketches for the building included enough detail to show sculptors what he had in mind, and he even designed the landscape, indicating where trees should be planted to serve as a backdrop for several sculptures. The building and grounds today look much like the early drawings from Pope's firm.

The architect asked James Earle Fraser, with whom he had worked on memorials in New York and Washington, to produce the sculpture for the Constitution Avenue side of the building, and he offered the Pennsylvania Avenue work to Adolph Alexander Weinman, who had sculpted two large Sphinx sculptures for Pope's Scottish Rite Temple in Washington. Both sculptors were already working on other buildings in the Federal Triangle project,

as well as on the U.S. Supreme Court Building. Because of the heavy workload, Weinman agreed to produce only the pediment on Pennsylvania Avenue. Pope then offered the rest of the work on that side of the building to Robert I. Aitken. The third sculptor also was very busy working on a pediment for the Supreme Court Building but took on the Archives as well. The sculptors oversaw the design and modeling of the sculptures, which were then cut in place by commercial stone carvers.

Though Fraser was the chief sculptor for the Constitution Avenue decorations, he subcontracted out a lot of the work, including the modeling of the pediment, an assignment he gave to his most trusted colleague—his wife Laura Gardin Fraser, who was a highly respected

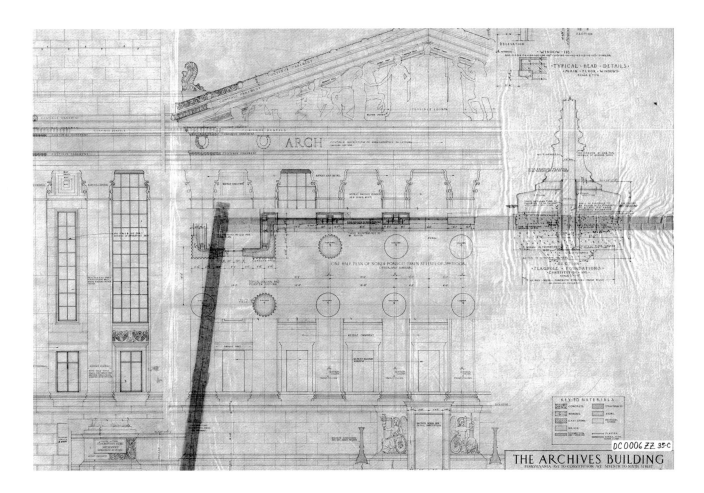

ARCH

THE ARCHIVES BUILDING
PENNSYLVANIA AVE TO CONSTITUTION AVE SEVENTH TO NINTH STREET

DC 0006 ZZ 35-C

AT RIGHT: **"The Recorder of the Archives"** pediment, designed by James and Laura Fraser, decorates the building's Constitution Avenue entrance and represents the archival process. The Recorder sits with a book in his lap and holds the keys to the Archives.

sculptor in her own right. Though other sculptors of the time rarely gave credit to their modelers, Fraser was known for acknowledging them. He had Laura Fraser's name, as well as the names of his other modelers, chiseled into the Archives Building sculptures along with his own.

The Frasers' "Recorder of the Archives" pediment is an allegorical representation of the archival process. The Zeus-like Recorder sits with a book in his lap and holds the keys to the Archives. His throne rests on rams, symbolizing parchment, which is made from animal skin, while the flower of the papyrus plant, symbolizing paper, decorates a frieze on the throne. Male figures stand and receive documents and female figures stand in front of Pegasus, the mythological winged horse

symbolizing inspiration. Dogs in the corners of the pediment—including some that Laura Fraser modeled after the couple's own beloved pets—represent guardianship of the treasured records. Laura Fraser visited the site often as her pediment was being carved, and while it was rare for sculptors to pick up the carving tools when it came to the final product, she did do some of the actual carving herself.

The freestanding "Heritage" sculpture, designed by Fraser and modeled by David K. Rubins, symbolizes the Government's role in preserving the home. A bare-breasted woman holds a nude baby boy and a sheaf of wheat, symbolizing a new generation and growth. In the woman's left hand is an urn, symbolizing the ashes of past generations. Draped over her shoulder is a

robe with a snake along its border—evoking the protection of the goddess Athena. Beneath, the inscription—a quotation attributed to then-Vice President John Garner—reads: "The heritage of the past is the seed that brings forth the harvest of the future." Pope designed the accompanying reliefs on the pedestal, which include a plow, a cornucopia, a lamp, and books, all symbolizing the importance of the home. The base also includes carvings of a winged globe with the United States front and center, an ox and a horse.

The "Guardianship" sculpture, designed by Fraser and modeled by Sidney B. Waugh, shows a muscular, semi-clothed man with a plumed helmet, symbolizing protection, in his right hand. On his left arm is a shield; in his hand a sword and fasces, symbolizing a unified government and the order it brings. A lion skin, evoking the god Hercules, hangs down the side of his chair, symbolizing strength and vigilance. Fraser selected the quote beneath this sculpture: "Eternal vigilance is the price of liberty." The quote is often attributed to Thomas Jefferson, but also has been attributed to the abolitionist Wendell Phillips who used it in a speech in 1852, and to Andrew Jackson, who said something very similar in his farewell address in 1837. The pedestal reliefs on the sculpture were added by Pope—a quiver of arrows, a strongbox, sword, and shield symbolizing protection.

Fraser also was responsible for 6 of the 13 attic medallions, representing the Departments of War, State, Treasury, Navy, Commerce, and Interior. For these, he simply had a model

strike different poses and photographed him, turning the photos over to Ulysses A. Ricci, who produced the designs.

On the opposite side of the building, Weinman designed the pediment "Destiny." Eagles atop fasces, symbolizing strength in unity, flank a central figure, Destiny. Eagles were used as a national icon of the United States but also to symbolize "lofty courage." Two winged genii—guardian spirits in Roman mythology—are carved above. To one side, a farmer on a horse is accompanied by a woman carrying a staff used in spinning wool, indicating the work of women and men in building the nation. The woman also carries branches of olive and palm, symbolizing victory and peace. Together, they symbolize the "arts of peace," while soldier figures on the other side symbolize the "arts of war." The figures to the far left are a wise man, a woman carrying the torch of enlightenment, a child carrying a garland of flowers, and a kneeling man with a harp, singing "The Song of Achievement." On the opposite side, two philosophers contemplating a skull, a kneeling figure, and a child with a scroll symbolize the "romance of history." On each end of the pediment, griffins guard "the secrets of the Archives." The theme of the pediment is that the future of the nation will be determined by the knowledge of the past as recorded by documents in the Archives.

While better known for their architectural sculpture, several artists who worked on the Archives Building also were successful coin designers.

STATE

MEDALLIONS

‖‖‖

Surrounding the attic frieze
are 13 medallions, each 8 feet
in diameter. The medallions
represent the 10 Cabinet-
level executive departments
at the time: Labor, Interior,
Commerce, Navy, Treasury,
State, War, Agriculture, Justice
and the Postal Service. The
Pennsylvania Avenue side of
the building also includes
medallions depicting the
Great Seal of the United States,
the U.S. Senate, and the U.S.
House of Representatives.

‖‖‖

Weinman designed the "Winged Liberty (Mercury) Dime" as well as the "Walking Liberty Half-Dollar." Aitken designed $50 gold octagonal and round coins in honor of the Panama-Pacific International Exposition. James Fraser designed the "Indian Head (or Buffalo) Nickel." Laura Gardin Fraser was the first woman to design a coin for the United States. She produced several commemorative coins, including a popular design for the quarter commemorating the 200th anniversary of George Washington's birth. She easily won the design competition judged by the Commission of Fine Arts and the Washington Bicentennial Commission, but Treasury Secretary Andrew Mellon refused to accept the result and insisted on another design by John Flanagan. Mellon left office before the controversy was resolved, and his successor Ogden Mills allowed the Flanagan design to be coined, saying the competition had been purely advisory.

Aitken, meanwhile, produced the "Guardians of the Portal" reliefs at the Pennsylvania Avenue entrance, seven attic medallions depicting the seal of the United States, the U.S. House of Representatives, the U.S. Senate, the U.S. Postal Service, and the Departments of Labor, Justice, and Agriculture, as well as the two freestanding sculptures on Pennsylvania Avenue:

In "The Past," an elderly, bearded philosopher sits with a scroll in his hand and the closed "book of history" in his lap as he stares "down the corridors of time." The quotation "Study the Past" is attributed to the Chinese philosopher Confucius, who said, "Study the past if you would divine

NAVY

WAR

AGRICULTURE

COMMERCE

LABOR

|||||||||||||||||||||||||||||||||||||||||||||||||||||||||||||||||||

Aitken's Department of
Labor medallion, on the
Pennsylvania Avenue side of
the building, was criticized
by the Commission of Fine
Arts, which recommended
that he go back and properly
connect the worker's neck and
shoulders. Perhaps because of
time constraints, the change
was never made.

|||||||||||||||||||||||||||||||||||||||||||||||||||||||||||||||||||

the future." On the base are carved symbols of strength and stability—shields, fasces, and an anchor—along with rams and eagles. Also featured prominently on the base is a depiction of Mercury, the Roman messenger god with wings on his head and a staff of intertwining snakes. He symbolizes wisdom and communication skills and appears in several places around the building.

In "The Future," a young woman with an open book gazes into the future. Beneath her, the inscription reads: "What is past is prologue," a quotation from Shakespeare's play *The Tempest*. On the base are carvings depicting the arts and sciences, including books and a lyre, as well as an urn symbolizing the past, eagles, torches and swords.

Inside the building, Pope concentrated most of the sculptural decoration on the Rotunda, which was to serve as a public gallery for viewing the Archives' most treasured documents: The Declaration of Independence, the Constitution of the United States, and the Bill of Rights.

Guarding the Rotunda are spear-topped gates decorated with griffins and numerous heads. It's unclear whether these are meant to be depictions of Mercury, the messenger god featured outside the building, or Medusa, the protector from Greek mythology with her distinctive hair of snakes, since Medusa also sometimes appears with wings or a bird in her hair. The Rotunda also includes at least nine eagles, numerous animal skulls, perhaps representing the past, and decorative rosettes.

Owl, lamp, soldier's helmet symbolizing
knowledge, protection

Mercury / Medusa shield

Soldier's armor symbolizing protection

AT LEFT: At first glance, Pope's Rotunda appears to have a full, domed ceiling, but it is, in fact, a half dome.

FOLLOWING SPREAD: Pope designed the Rotunda as a shrine for the nation's founding documents.

The swastika—most familiar today as the political symbol of Nazi Germany but actually used by many cultures around the world—is found throughout the Archives Building. The symbol runs around the exterior of the building, borders the bronze doors on the Constitution Avenue entrance, and surrounds a bronze circular design embedded in the floor of the foyer leading to the Rotunda. The floor design includes medallions and four winged figures symbolizing Legislation, Justice, History, and War and Defense. Records on all of those subjects are contained within the Archives.

The Rotunda murals were painted in oil by Barry Faulkner, a well-known muralist who also produced works for bank buildings, state capitals, and New York's Rockefeller Center.

The two murals above the Charters of Freedom and other glass-enclosed documents depict the presentation of the Declaration of Independence to John Hancock, president of the Continental Congress, and the presentation of the U.S. Constitution by James Madison to George Washington, president of the Constitutional Convention. In both murals, the scenes are imagined by the artist. In reality, the people depicted were never in the room at the same time for any dramatic presentation of the documents that forged the nation.

Faulkner received $36,000 for the murals and was given two years to complete them with his team of painters. He complained his knowledge of history was "inadequate" to select the statesmen to be included and sought the

N   OF   INDEPENDE

TUTION OF THE UN

PREVIOUS SPREAD: **Details from Barry Faulkner's murals in the Rotunda. At left, Thomas Jefferson delivers the finished draft of the Declaration of Independence. At right, George Washington is presented with the U.S. Constitution.**

advice of Dr. J. Franklin Jameson, a respected historian at the Library of Congress who had pushed to create the National Archives. Jameson gave the artist a list of statesmen from each of the 13 states and other figures who had been influential at the conventions that produced the documents. Working from portraits and woodcuts of the Founders as well as historical descriptions about their height, coloring, and wardrobe, Faulkner costumed and posed live models, and then he and his assistants spent a year making small sketches of each person, then a small-scale color rendering of the murals, before beginning to paint the huge canvasses.

Rather than placing the delegates in Independence Hall in Philadelphia where the conventions were held, Faulkner designed a landscape background using the skies to increase the drama of the murals. The sky in the Declaration of Independence mural is dark and stormy, symbolizing its adoption in the midst of war, while the Constitution of the United States mural's sky is peaceful, symbolizing the hope inherent in forging a new nation and a new government.

Well-known Revolutionary battle flags are depicted in the Declaration mural; the Constitution mural flags are those of the original 13 states, symbolizing the formation of the union.

The murals, each measuring 14 by 36 feet, were painted in a large rented space in New York's Grand Central Station, near the door to catwalks used to change the light bulbs over the plaster dome of the train station's concourse. Faulkner said he and his three assistants took their breaks on the catwalk, enjoying the darkness after painting under a bright light. Once the paintings were finished, the muralist hosted a large cocktail party at the studio.

The canvasses were sent to Washington in the fall of 1936. "The recesses of the Archives were cool and I watched with intense excitement the 'paper hangers' unroll the canvasses on the slightly curving wall," Faulkner wrote. "Each was a few inches too short." Faulkner and his assistants fixed this by adding foliage to the edges of the paintings in place. The murals are among the largest single-piece oil-on-canvas murals in the country.

JUSTICE

Architect John Russell Pope designed the Archives Building as a temple to American history. In the floor of the entryway to the Rotunda, he placed a decorative bronze medallion with symbolic representations of the functions of Government, including "Justice," right.

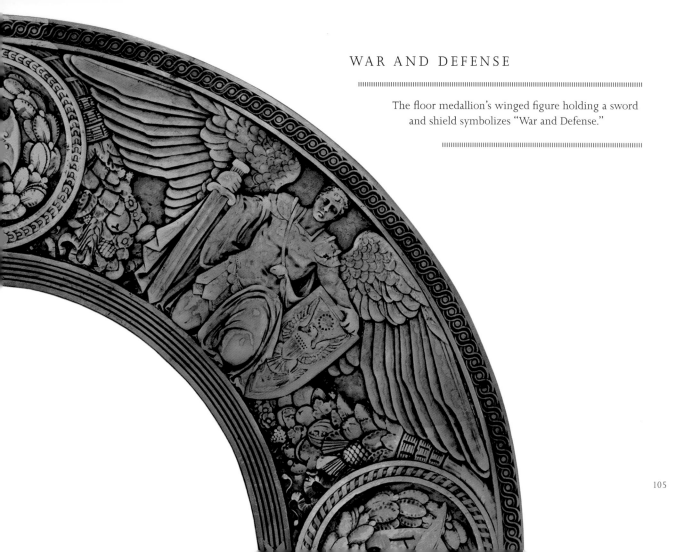

WAR AND DEFENSE

The floor medallion's winged figure holding a sword
and shield symbolizes "War and Defense."

HISTORY

The winged figure holding a quill pen, book, and globe, right, symbolizes "History."

LEGISLATION

The winged figure clutching the "Senate" tablet
and the fasces, along with the depiction of the
Ten Commandments, center, symbolize
"Legislation," or the origins of law.

MERCURY OR MEDUSA?

The Roman messenger god
Mercury, with wings on his
head and a staff of intertwining snakes, symbolizes
wisdom and communication
skills. But Medusa, the protector from Greek mythology
with a hair of snakes—the one
who turns you to stone if you
meet her gaze—also some-
times appears with wings or a
bird in her hair. Like Mercury,
she also often appears on
a shield because the god-
dess Athena used her as a
scary symbol to ward off her
enemies. It's unclear whether
the carvings inside and
outside the Archives Building
are Mercury or Medusa, or
whether different sculptors
intended different things.

FASCES

Fasces are a bundle of sticks or rods tied together, sometimes with an executioner's ax in the middle. The symbol from ancient Rome signifies government authority, and has come to symbolize the unity and strength of many working together. Italian Fascism took its name from the fasces. In the Archives Building, look for fasces everywhere.

DOGS

‖‖‖

As "man's best friends," dogs
are associated with loyalty as
well as with guardianship and
vigilance. Laura Fraser used
dogs in each corner of the
"Recorder of the Archives"
Pediment on Constitution
Avenue, including some modeled after her own pets.

‖‖‖

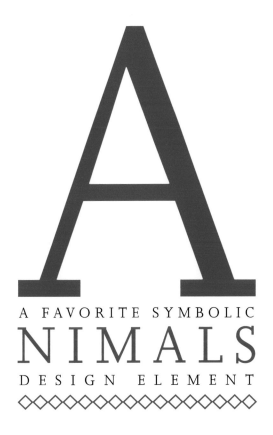

A FAVORITE SYMBOLIC

NIMALS

DESIGN ELEMENT

EAGLES

‖‖‖

The national symbol of the United States, the eagle also signifies freedom, strength, and courage. There are numerous eagles incorporated into the sculptural design on the exterior of the building, including 12-foot-tall eagles on each end of the pediments. There are at least nine eagles in the interior Rotunda.

‖‖‖

RAMS

|||||||||||||||||||||||||||||||||||||||||||||||||||||||||||

Rams appear in several sculptures as well as on light stands inside and out-side the building. They are a symbol for parchment, which is made from animal skin and was used to record the nation's earliest laws and treaties.

|||||||||||||||||||||||||||||||||||||||||||||||||||||||||||

HORSES / PEGASUS

|||||||||||||||||||||||||||||||||||||||||||||||||||||||||||

Horses typically symbolize noble strength and power. The mythological winged horse Pegasus, used in the "Recorder of the Archives" pediment, symbolizes magical inspiration.

|||||||||||||||||||||||||||||||||||||||||||||||||||||||||||

LIONS

‖‖‖

Lions, as well as lion skins
and paws, are often associated with the god Hercules
and signify strength,
power, and vigilance. A
lion's skin appears in the
"Guardianship" sculpture
and lion heads decorate the
exterior attic frieze. Lion's
paws also decorate light
posts around the building.

‖‖‖

DOLPHINS

Dolphins, known for their intelligence and friendliness toward humans, appear on light stands outside the Pennsylvania Avenue entrance to the building. In Greek mythology, dolphins are associated with Apollo, who once took the form of a dolphin, and with the god of the seas, Poseidon.

OWLS

|||||||||||||||||||||||||||||||||||||||||||||||||||||||||||||||

Owls like those carved on
the 7th and 9th Street sides
of the building symbol-
ize wisdom, knowledge,
and learning. Because owls
see well at night, they also
symbolize vigilance and
guardianship.

|||||||||||||||||||||||||||||||||||||||||||||||||||||||||||||||

GRIFFINS

The griffin, used in Weinman's "Destiny" pediment on Pennsylvania Avenue, as well as on the gates inside the Rotunda, and even on some lighting sconces elsewhere in the building, is a mythological animal with the head and wings of an eagle and the body of a lion. To ancient Greeks, the griffin symbolized vigilant strength. Griffins were said to guard the gold of the mythological Hyperborea. Here, they guard the treasures of the Archives.

PAST

(letters forming "PEACE" "SURE" overlaid)

"THE PAST, AT LEAST, IS SECURE."

Daniel Webster

(Proposed inscription for the National Archives Building Rotunda)

123

PAGE 122: A human skull in the "Destiny" pediment on Pennsylvania Avenue symbolizes the past.

SOMETHING'S MISSING

Pope's design for the National Archives Building called for numerous statues and carved inscriptions inside and out, but Depression-era cost-cutting thwarted some of his plans while his Government clients rejected others as redundant or ill-conceived. If it looks like something is missing, chances are it was never there in the first place. *Look for these examples:*

• In four places on the exterior of the building, rectangular portions of walls are framed in, giving the appearance of empty picture frames or windows later blocked. Two are on the Constitution Avenue side of the building, and the others are on the south ends of 7th and 9th Streets. These were intended to showcase chiseled inscriptions listing the Federal Government agencies whose records would form the contents of the Archives Building. The planned inscriptions were omitted at the last minute because Government planners realized they would soon be out of date as the Federal Government would continue to grow and add more departments whose records also would flow into the National Archives.

• Scrolls beneath the carved owls on the building's east and west sides are blank. It's unclear whether the architect intended to have text inscribed on these.

• Inside the building, a blank, framed-in wall greets visitors on the west side of the Pennsylvania Avenue entrance. A planned inscription was to list the name of the architect, the President of the United States, and other officials involved in the building project. It was rejected because a similar inscription was to appear at the Constitution Avenue entrance. As it turned out, the inscription appears in neither place. The original inscription planned for the east wall of the Pennsylvania Avenue entrance was to read: "A repository for the important documents of the Federal Government … the laws and treaties of the early republic … the records which relate to the establishment of national policies and the authoritative sources for research in the various phases of the development of the American nation." This inscription was approved, but never inscribed, perhaps for budgetary reasons.

• In the Rotunda, four statuary alcoves stand vacant, as they have since the building opened. Neoclassical buildings typically include statues of Greek or Roman gods and goddesses, such as those in Pope's building down the street from the National Archives, the National Gallery of Art (West Building). It is unclear what statues Pope intended to place in the Rotunda niches. The architect's description of the space said only that the decorations and materials used in the Rotunda would be "in keeping with its purpose and character."

• The bronze panel over the Constitution Avenue entrance to the Rotunda also is missing something—a quote from Daniel Webster that was approved, but never carved: "The past, at least, is secure."

ACKNOWLEDGMENTS

This book would not have been possible had it not been for the contributions of time, talent, and creativity of many individuals.

The book project was conceived by Thora Colot, executive director of the Foundation for the National Archives, and was managed by the Foundation's publications and research manager Christina Gehring. Franck Cordes, director of administration and marketing, provided valuable insight into the symbolic imagery of the building.

I would also like to thank our copyeditor, Maureen MacDonald of the National Archives and Records Administration, as well as the Archives' Rick Blondo and Bruce Bustard, who lent their expertise on the building, provided their own research as a starting point for the book, and read the first drafts.

The bulk of the beautiful contemporary photographs in the book were taken by Carol Highsmith and Colin Winterbottom, and Lance Rutter and Yann Legendre deserve all credit and my thanks for the book's elegant design.

In addition, I would like to thank the following individuals, who provided key information, photographs, and feedback that made all the difference:

From the National Archives and Records Administration:
Acting Archivist of the United States Adrienne Thomas, Sam Anthony, Jackie Budell, Susan Cooper, Suzanne Isaacs, Earl McDonald, Tom Nastick, Nick Natanson, Marvin Pinkert, Lee Ann Potter, Rodney Ross, Chris Smith, Richard Smith, and Debra Wall.

From the Franklin Delano Roosevelt Presidential Library and Museum:
Bob Clark

From the Supreme Council Ancient & Accepted Scottish Rite, Southern Jurisdiction, U.S.A.:
Arturo de Hoyos and Larissa Watkins

From the National Gallery of Art, Washington, DC:
Jean Henry, Gallery Archives

From the National Park Service:
Terry J. Adams

I am very appreciative of everyone who has been a part of *The National Archives Building: Temple of American History*. Thank you all.

Patty Reinert Mason

PHOTO CREDITS

The items reproduced in this book, except where noted, were selected from the holdings of the National Archives and Records Admininistration. They are identified by record group name and number or by still picture number.

Cover, pp. 4, 15, 56, 78, 89, 109–110, 112, 114, 117, 121–122, photos courtesy of Colin Winterbottom; p. 8, Records of the Public Buildings Service, RG 121: CEDIS, DC0006ZZ #25; p. 10, 64-NA-136; p. 16, 64-NAD-48; p. 18, 64-NAD-63; p. 20, General Records of the U.S. Government, RG 11; p. 23, photo courtesy of Arturo de Hoyos, Grand Archivist, the Supreme Council, 33°, Southern Jurisdiction, U.S.A.; p. 24, RG 121: Advisory Committee for the National Archives Building, #57; p. 26, Library of Congress; p. 31, RG 121: CEDIS, DC0006ZZ #29; pp. 32–34, RG 121: CEDIS, DC0006ZZ #39; pp. 36, 38, 42–43, 45, 72–75, 79, 83–87, 90, 92–93, 95–96, 98–101, 104–108, 111,115–116, 118, photos courtesy of Carol M. Highsmith; pp. 39, 76, 119–120, photos by Earl McDonald; p. 46, 66-G-23L-47; p. 48, 64-NA-71; p. 49, 64-NA-273a; p. 51, 83-G-3653; p. 52, 83-G-21; p. 55, 121-BCP-111A-80; p. 58, 121-BCP-111B-47; p. 61, 200-EAS-E-11; p. 62, 121-BCP-111B-40; p. 63, 121-BCP-111C-69; p. 64, 121-BCP-111C-88; p. 67, 121-BCP-111C-95; p. 68, 64-NAC-280; p. 69, 121-BA-3977-1; p. 70, 64-CP-F-150; p. 71, photo by Franck Cordes; p. 81, RG 121: CEDIS, DC0006ZZ #35; p. 103, 64-NA-1-148.